LIHE

POPCORN

POP SONGS
TO PLAY AND SING

TIM NORELL
&
ULF WAHLBERG

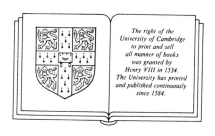

The right of the
University of Cambridge
to print and sell
all manner of books
was granted by
Henry VIII in 1534.
The University has printed
and published continuously
since 1584.

CAMBRIDGE UNIVERSITY PRESS

Cambridge

New York   New Rochelle

Melbourne   Sydney

Published by the Press Syndicate of the University of Cambridge
The Pitt Building, Trumpington Street, Cambridge CB2 1RP
32 East 57th Street, New York, NY 10022, USA
10 Stamford Road, Oakleigh, Melbourne 3166, Australia

Originally published in Swedish as *Pop-korn* by Almqvist & Wiksell Läromedel AB, Stockholm 1980
and © Tim Norell, Ulf Wahlberg and Almqvist & Wiksell Läromedel AB, Stockholm 1980
First published in English as *Popcorn* by Cambridge University Press 1983

Printed in Great Britain at the University Press, Cambridge

ISBN 0 521 28931 9

Thanks are due to Kristina Gemzell for her collaboration in the translation from the
Swedish original.

Cover design: Robin Lawrie

WD

Contents

Introduction

Popcorn is a collection of some of the songs of the seventies (or late sixties) that have become pop history. But it is more than that: it offers schools a way of bringing the pop idiom into the classroom. It provides pupils with the opportunity for active involvement in playing and singing pop music rather than just passive listening.

The songs (all with at least a melody line and guitar chords) have been chosen not just because they are — or have been — popular and successful, but also to fulfil the following criteria:

*the song should be easy to sing

*the pitch should be suitable for 13 to 16-year-olds

*the music and chord charts should be easy to read.

There is background information (notes and photographs) on the singers, groups and composers.

Some practical suggestions

Many of the songs in *Popcorn* contain quite a wide variety of parts to play. For example, 'Sailing' on page 14 has a bass tune and bass accompaniment in addition to the melody part with guitar chords; the chord diagrams on page 15 make it easy to learn the chords and to make a rhythmical chord accompaniment. There is a full chord chart at the end of the book.

Examples of how to add a piano chord accompaniment with the help of the chord charts are given with some songs. Other songs include parts of the introduction and instrumental interludes taken from the original recording.

The music for guitar is always written one octave higher than it sounds. When tuning guitars to the piano, the highest string of the guitar corresponds to the E above middle C.

Bass accompaniment

Ideally groups playing these songs should have a bass guitar or double bass. The frets and convenient size of the bass guitar, make it easy to handle — and of course, it's perfect for pop music. The bass tune of 'Sailing' is written so that all the notes except one can be played on open strings. The difficult note is B, which can be obtained by pressing the A-string on the second fret on the fingerboard of the bass guitar. If you have a double bass, the position can be marked with a coloured sticker. The instruments are tuned like this:

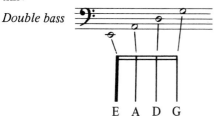

Double bass

E A D G

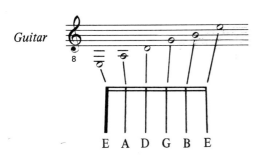

Guitar

E A D G B E

Drums

Drums are important in all pop music. If there isn't a drummer available, the drumming can still be provided if the set of drums is divided between several players. (This will work well with most of the songs in the book.)

One pupil plays the 1st and the 3rd beat in the bar on a bass drum:

Another plays the 2nd and the 4th on a snare drum:

Another pupil can play semi-quavers fairly softly with a drumstick on closed hi-hat or with a whisk on a cymbal:

If there is no drum-set available the rhythm can be played on a hand-drum, tambourine and cymbal.

You are the sunshine of my life

Words and music: Stevie Wonder

You are the sun—shine of—— my life——
You are the ap——ple of—— my eye——

That's why I'll al——ways be a - round——
For - ev - er you'll—— stay in my heart——

I feel like this—— is the —— be - gin - ning——

though I've loved you—— for a mil—— lion years——

And if I thought— our love— was end - ing—— I'd

find my self— drown—— ing in my own tears.—— Whoa,—— whoa——

2 You are the sunshine of my life,
   that's why I'll always stay around.
   You are the apple of my eye.
   Forever you'll stay in my heart.

   You must have known that I was lonely,
   because you came to my rescue.
   And I know that this must be heaven,
   how could so much love be inside of you?
   Whoa, whoa . . .

   You are the sunshine . . .

D7/C The letter after the oblique indicates an alternative bass note.

Example of piano accompaniment

STEVIE WONDER

Stevie Wonder, who has been blind from birth, says that 'a handicap isn't a handicap unless you make it one', and you are certainly not aware of any handicap when you're listening to Stevie's music.

He was born in 1950 in the USA, in Saginaw, Michigan. His interest in music developed early; it led him to study music in Braille, and so his feeling for rhythm and melody developed at a young age. At twelve he made his first record, which was a smash hit in the USA. It was followed by several others such as: 'You are the sunshine of my life' and 'Songs in the key of life'.

Stevie has developed a style of his own. It could be described as melodious soul music – melody is very important in his music, a fact that becomes clear when you listen to his songs.

Streets of London

Words and music: Ralph McTell

Have you seen the old man in the closed down mar-ket,
kick-ing up the pa-pers with his worn out shoes?
In his eyes you see no pride, hand held loose-ly by his side—
Yes-ter-day's pa-per tell-ing yes-ter-day's news— So
how can you tell me you're lone- - ly and say for you—
that the sun don't shine— Let me take— you
by the hand— and lead you through the streets of Lon-don. I'll show you
some-thing to make you change your mind. mind.

2 Have you seen the old girl
   who walks the streets of London.
   Dirt in her hair and her clothes in rags?
   She's no time for talkin'
   She just keeps right on walkin',
   Carrying her home in two carrier bags.

   So how can you tell me . . .

3 In the all night café
   at a quarter past eleven
   Same old man sitting there on his own.
   Looking at the world over the rim of his teacup
   Each tea lasts an hour and he wanders home alone.

   So how can you tell me . . .

8

Second tune of the refrain

So how can you tell me you're lone - ly and say for you that the sun don't shine—— Let me take— you by the hand— and lead you through the streets of London. I'll show you something to make you change your mind.

4 Have you seen the old man
outside the seaman's mission,
Memory fading with the medal ribbon that he wears?
In our winter city the rain cries a little pity
For one more forgotten hero and a world that doesn't care.

So how can you tell me . . .

RALPH McTELL

As a child, Ralph lived in post-war London with his mother and younger brother, in an environment which was anything but luxurious. As a teenager he took various jobs such as waiter, barman, gardener in different parts of England.

In 1966, he met the guitarist and singer, Wizz Jones, and moved to Cornwall where he wrote his first songs. In November of that year he went to Norway, where he wrote his greatest hit, 'Streets of London'.

9

How deep is your love

Words and music: B. Gibb — R. Gibb — M. Gibb

Note that the end of the verse goes into the beginning of the refrain.

THE BEE GEES

The three Gibb brothers: Barry, Maurice and Robin, who call themselves the Bee Gees, originally come from Australia, where they made a reputation for themselves as musicians and composers early in their career. They made their first recordings as early as 1962.

In 1967, the Bee Gees moved to England and there they produced the record 'Spicks and Specks', which rapidly became Number One in the English charts. A large number of other hits followed this, and as a result the Bee Gees became known all over the world.

In 1969, the brothers decided to split up. Barry and Maurice went on making records together while Robin opted for a solo career. At the end of 1970, the brothers joined up again and decided to take the world by storm once more – as the Bee Gees. They made a large number of records, several of which became great hits, but the real breakthrough that proved the Bee Gees were really a force to be reckoned with came when the brothers did the music for the film 'Saturday Night Fever'.

11

Walk right in

Words and music: Cannon — Wood

1. Walk right in— set right— down— Dad - dy let your mind roll on———
2. Walk right in— set right— down— Ba - by let your hair hang down———

Walk right in— set right down— Daddy, let your mind roll on———
Walk right in— set right down— Ba - by, let your hair hang down———

Ev - 'ry - body's talk-ing 'bout a new way o' walk-in'— Do you want a lose— your

mind? Walk right in— set right— down Daddy, let your mind roll on———

Ba - by, let your hair hang down——— Walk right in—

set right— down— Ba - by let your hair— hang— down.

Bass tune Open strings. In two bars the bass tunes or the open strings are in brackets — it is obviously preferable for the upper notes to be played.

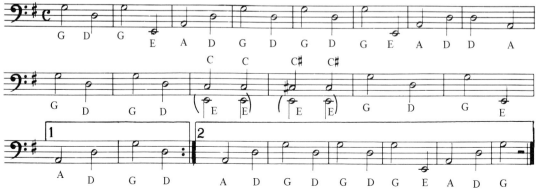

12

The house of the rising sun

Traditional

There is a house in New Or - leans, they call the Ris - ing Sun. And it's
been the ru - in of ma - ny—— a poor boy, and God, I know—— I'm one.

My mo - ther was a tai - lor————
on - ly thing a gamb - ler——needs, is a

Sewed my new blue jeans. My fa - ther was a gam - blin man
suit - case and a trunk. And the on - ly time he'll be satis - fied, is

down in New - Or - leans. Now the . . . Oh, . . .
when he's all a - drunk.

2 Oh! Mother tell your children
not to do what I have done.
Spend your lives in sin and misery,
in the house of the Rising Sun.

Well, I've got one foot on the platform.
The other foot on the train.
I'm going back to New Orleans,
to wear that ball and chain.

Well, there is a house in New Orleans
they call the Rising Sun.
And it's been the ruin of many a poor boy,
and God, I know I'm one.

Sailing

Words and music: Gavin Sunderland

I am sail - ing, I am sail - ing, home a - gain— 'cross the
fly - ing, I am fly - ing, like a bird— 'cross the

sea. I am sail—— ing stor - my wa - ters To be
sky. I am fly—— ing pass - ing high clouds, To be

near—— you to be free. I am. . .
with—— you to be free. Can you. . . Oh Lord— to be

near—— you To be free. Oh Lord— to be

3 Can you hear me, Can you hear me,
Thro' the dark night far away.
I am dying, forever trying
to be with you, who can say.

4 We are sailing, We are sailing,
home again 'cross the sea.
We are sailing, Stormy waters,
to be near you, to be free.
Oh Lord to be near you, to be free.

ROD STEWART

Rod Stewart was born in London of Scottish
parents. He started his career as a singer in the mid
1960s when he sang with various bands around
London. In 1967 he was invited to become a
singer in the guitarist Jeff Beck's group. He took
up the offer and made two LPs which were highly
acclaimed by the critics.

In 1969 he formed a new group called 'The
Faces'. The group rapidly became immensely
popular in England and had a few hits around the
world as well. While working with 'The Faces',
Rod recorded for Mercury and at the same time
carried on a solo career with hits such as 'Maggie
May', 'Gasoline Alley' and 'Sailing'.

Bass

Open D-string   Second fret on   Open G-string   Open D-string   Open E-string   Second fret on
                A string   A-string

Open E-string   Open D, open A   Open D, open A   Open E-string   Open D-string, open A-string

Guitar sequences

The oblique signs indicate taps on the strings. The sequence contains one bar chord (Bm).

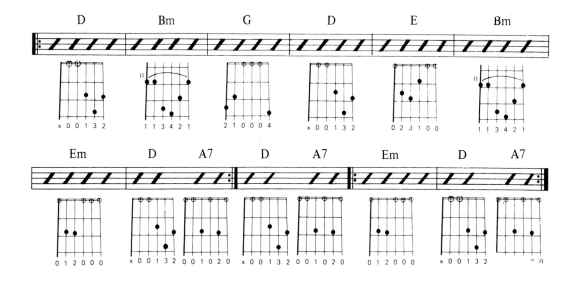

Border song

Words and music: Elton John — Bernie Taupin

Piano introduction

Ho - ly Mo - ses I have been re - moved——.

I have seen the spec——-tre. He has been here— too——.

Distant cou-sin from down—— the line—— Brand of people who ain't——

—-. my kind—— Ho - ly Mo - ses, I have been re - moved—,

Piano   Piano

I'm go - ing back to the bor - der where my af - fairs—— where

my af - fairs— ain't— a - bused——. I can't— take a - ny more— bad wa——ter. Been

poi - soned from my head down to my shoes——. Oh,——. Piano

He's my brother let us live in peace—— Oh——— let us live

let— us live— in peace. Piano

2 Holy Moses, I have been deceived.
Now the wind has changed direction
and I have to leave.
Won't you please excuse my frankness,
but it's not my cup of tea.

Holy Moses, I have been deceived.
I'm going back to the border,
where my affairs, where my affairs
aint't abused.

3 Holy Moses, let us live in peace.
Let us strive to find a way to
make all hatred cease.
There's a man over there.
What's his colour, I don't care.
He's my brother. Let us live,
let us live in peace. Oh——
He's my brother
let us live, let us live
in peace.

ELTON JOHN

There have been many attempts to
combine poetry, orchestral music
and rock. In some cases these have
been successful, in others they
haven't. Elton John who, together
with lyric-writer Bernie Taupin, has
composed a lot of hits (among
them several regarded as pop
classics) is among those who've
been successful in this attempt.
Elton John's music is characterized
by its softness, and by melodies
played in a 'funky' way. His
method of playing the piano has
set a trend all over the world. His
odd choice of clothes and above
all his glasses have made him a
popular subject for the media.

Let it be

Words and music: John Lennon — Paul McCartney

When I find my-self— in times of trouble Mother Ma——ry comes to me Speaking words of wis———-dom, let it be.— And in my hour of dark———-ness She is standing right in front of me Speaking words of wis———-dom let it be.— Let it be— let it be——— Let it be——— let it be— Whisper words of wis———-dom, let it be——— And when. . .— Let it be——— let it be— let it be——— let it be——— Whis-per words of wis-dom, let it be———

Chorus parts in the refrain

18

2 And when the broken hearted people,
  living in the world agree.
  There will be an answer, let it be.
  For though they may get parted, there is
  still a chance that they will see.
  There will be an answer, let it be.

  Let it be, let it be, let it be, let it be
  There will be an answer, let it be.

3 And when the night is cloudy,
  there is still a light that shines on me.
  Shine until tomorrow, let it be.
  I wake up to the sound of music,
  Mother Mary comes to me.
  Speaking words of wisdom, let it be.

  Let it be, let it be, let it be, let it be.
  Whisper words of wisdom, let it be.

  Let it be, let it be, let it be, let it be.
  Whisper words of wisdom, let it be.

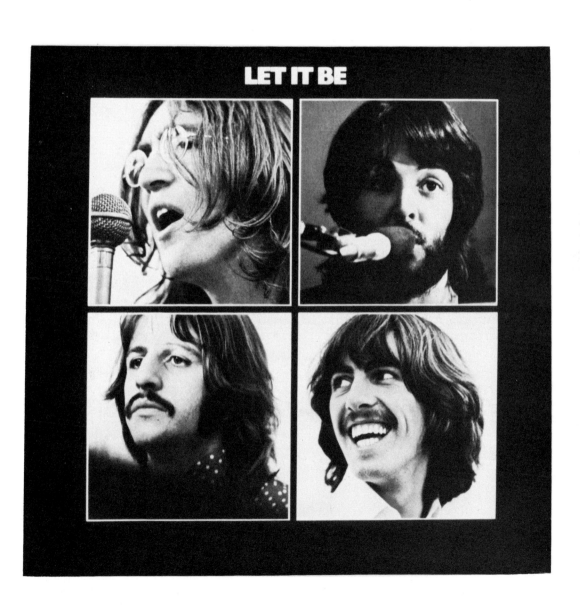

When I'm sixty-four

Words and music: John Lennon — Paul McCartney

When I get old—er los-ing my hair—— ma-ny years from now—

—— will you still be send-ing me a va-len-tine,—— birth-day greet-ings

bottle of wine.—— If I'd been out—— till quarter to three——

would you lock the door—— Will you still need— me will you still feed—— me

when I'm six-ty-four. 1 Oooo

2 Ev'-ry summer we can rent a cottage in the Isle of Wight——

—— if it's not too dear—— You'll be old - er too——

We shall scrimp and save——

Ah—— And if you say the word—— I could

Grand - children on your knee—— Ve - ra,

2nd time
D.C. al FINE

stay with you.
Chuck and Dave.

20

2 I could be handy, mending a fuse,
   when your lights have gone.
   You can knit a sweater by the fireside,
   Sunday mornings, go for a ride.

   Doing the garden, digging the weeds,
   who could ask for more.
   Will you still need me,
   will you still feed me,
   when I'm sixty-four.

   Ev'ry summer we can rent a
   cottage in the Isle of Wight
   if it's not too dear.
   We shall scrimp and save.
   Grandchildren on your knee,
   Vera, Chuck and Dave.

3 Send me a postcard, drop me a line,
   stating point of view.
   Indicate precisely what you
   mean to say,
   yours sincerely wasting away.

   Give me your answer, fill in a form,
   mine for evermore.
   Will you still need me,
   will you still feed me,
   when I'm sixty-four.

THE BEATLES

Today the Beatles are history. Their music is played everywhere and in widely varying styles. It can be heard in the guise of one-fingered accompaniments in bars, of hard-swinging jazz or of symphonic orchestra pieces.

The Beatles were formed in the late fifties by John Lennon, Paul McCartney, George Harrison and a drummer by the name of Pete Best, but in those days the band was called the 'Quarrymen'. In the early sixties, the band toured as 'The Silver Beatles' in Hamburg, where their playing routine was established. Already in 1961 Brian Epstein had come into the picture as their manager. The next year they signed their first record contract and in June 1962 the Beatles made their first test recordings. Soon afterwards Pete Best was sacked in favour of a new drummer – Ringo Starr.

In October their first record came out – the single 'Love Me Do'. Brian Epstein was pleased with the boys. He began to make them work and rehearse a new way. They let their hair grow and Epstein took charge of their style of dress and behaviour both on the stage and in private. In April 1963 the LP 'Please Please Me' came out. Tours and stage performances came thick and fast. The single 'She Loves You' came out in August and it rapidly became a hit.

In October the Beatles made a journey to Sweden where they made TV-programmes and gave a few performances – already signs of idol hysteria were in evidence among the fans. Back in England they took part in a televised concert at the London Palladium. Afterwards they were stormed and there was a near-riot. When the group gave a performance at the Royal Variety Show at the Prince of Wales Theatre, John introduced the first number with the words: 'The public on the cheapest seats applaud and you [with a glance at the Royal boxes] rattle your jewels.' Next day all the papers had Lennon's words on their front pages.

Then followed a successful tour of the USA, the making of the film 'A Hard Day's Night', and tours to Denmark, Hong Kong, Australia and New Zealand.
(Continued on next page)

Now the Beatles were established internationally. 'The Liverpool Sound' had reached out all over the world and the Beatles were the symbol of this music, which was regarded by many people as a musical revolution. 1966 turned out to be the Beatles' hardest year. A series of recordings were made. Paul and John composed hard. The pressure on the group from outside increased. They made a world tour which finished in San Francisco, where the group gave their last public performance together. Now they wanted to be left alone in peace. But they were perhaps the most carefully guarded and the most publicity-worthy people in the world and they had no chance of any private life. During the tours the boys sat like prisoners in their hotel rooms. They had to sit there, separated from the world and chained to each other. It was then that the real splits between them began to show. The strain became too much. They were already multi-millionaires and so it didn't matter to them how much they earned. Still they went on together with their work. The year 1967 was, if anything, to be as busy as the previous year. 'Sgt. Pepper's Lonely Hearts Club Band', an LP hailed by some as a work of genius, came out that year.

But it eventually became clear that the four of them were finding it increasingly difficult to work together, even if now and again they got together and produced good work. 1970 saw the last LP made under the name of the Beatles. It was called 'Let it be'. John Lennon went his own way together with his wife Yoko Ono until his death on 9 December 1980, at the hand of a gunman. Paul McCartney is working with his group Wings. George Harrison has developed as a composer and has gone in for a solo career. Ringo Starr is making records and doing film work as well.

Records by the Beatles

Please Please Me	Revolver
With the Beatles	Sgt. Pepper's Lonely Hearts Club Band
Beatles for Sale	Magical Mystery Tour
A Hard Day's Night	Beatles double album
Help	Yellow Submarine
Rubber Soul	Let it Be

My sweet Lord

Words and music: George Harrison

Ain't that just the way

Words and music: Belland — Larson — Phillips

NB should be sung an octave lower than shown!

2 Now he's in another place
and I can't reach him.
And I feel as though I'm
guilty of a crime.
I took all he had to give
and gave him nothin',
and all it would have taken
was some time.

Ain't that just the way that
life goes down, down, down, down.
Movin' way too fast or much too slow.
Gettin' up, gettin' high, gettin' down,
gettin' no, no, nowhere,
but not gettin' into
someone I should know.

BARBI BENTON

Barbi came to Hollywood in 1968 as a 19-year-old to study veterinary medicine. But she
soon became involved in the show-business life around her. She went to a theatre school
for three years and appeared in television advertisements. It was due to a brief television
appearance that the owner of 'Playboy', Hugh M. Hefner discovered Barbi and engaged
her as a 'beautiful girl in the background' in his own television show 'Playboy after Dark'.
She also worked as a bunny-girl in one of Hefner's nightclubs and appeared as a cover-girl
in 'Playboy' during 1973—74. The TV-chief Sam McCloud heard her singing in a television
programme and asked her to appear in an episode about a young actress in New York
who's fallen into the clutches of an unscrupulous record-king.

In this programme Barbi sang 'Ain't that just the way' and that's how she suddenly
became a name outside the USA.

You can get it if you really want

Words and music: Jimmy Cliff

Example of rhythm accompaniment

To illustrate the reggae rhythm (so-called off-beat)

Handclap

Stamp

Guitar chords

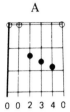

A

0 0 2 3 4 0

D

x 0 0 1 3 2

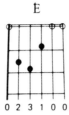

E

0 2 3 1 0 0

E7

0 2 0 1 4 0

JIMMY CLIFF

'You can get it if you really want' comes from a film called 'The harder they come'. The leading role in the film is played by Jimmy Cliff, who is one of Jamaica's greatest reggae singers.

Reggae, a typically Jamaican phenomenon, is a further development of calypso and rock. The main characteristic of reggae is that the rhythm is chopped up and the unstressed rhythm element forms the backbone of the music.

By the rivers of Babylon

Words and music: Farian — Reyam — Dowe — McNaughton

The lower part in unison parts can be sung one octave higher and it can also be used in the chorus.

BONEY M

Boney M is the name of one of the best-known disco-groups from Germany. The group consists of Lis Mitchell from Jamaica, Maizie Williams from the Canary Islands, Marcia Barrett, also from Jamaica, and the only boy in the group, Bobby Farrell. They have had a number of great hits as a group, for example 'Daddy Cool', 'No Woman No Cry' and 'By the Rivers of Babylon'.

Money, money, money

Words and music: Benny Andersson — Björn Ulvaeus

ABBA

The Swedish pop-group ABBA have achieved enormous success with their records all round the world.

ABBA was formed in 1972, but the four members had already worked in the music business for a long time before that. In the sixties, Björn and Benny were members of two of Sweden's most popular bands, Hootenanny Singers and Hep Stars. They already knew each other in those days and in 1966 they wrote their first song together. In 1967, Anni-Frid made her break-through as a solo artist and a year later Agneta topped the Swedish charts with a song of her own composition. At the same time, Björn and Benny left their respective groups and Agneta and Anni-Frid, Björn and Benny were launched as lyric artists with their own songs and Agneta and Anni-Frid sang as backing.

In 1972, the girls came into the foreground and the group 'Björn, Benny, Agneta and Anni-Frid' was formed. They stuck to that name until there was so much talk about the group that it began to seem too long and difficult to use. So each member's initial was taken and the group took on the name ABBA.

In 1973, the group took part in the Swedish selection for the Eurovision Song Contest, with their song 'Ring, Ring'. The Swedish jury turned it down but it was a hit both in Sweden and abroad.

In 1974 they had better luck. In Brighton, ABBA won the Eurovision Song Contest with 'Waterloo'. It was to be the first in a long series of major international hits. In 1975, the group toured in Sweden and they produced the LP 'ABBA'. In the same year the group went to the USA and made television programmes. In 1976 they went on tour to Australia where they received an incredible response. That same year the LP 'Arrival' was produced and sold over seven million copies all over the world. The next year the group came top of the American charts with 'Dancing Queen'.

At Christmas, 1977, their first film 'ABBA – The Movie' had its première and at the same time the music was produced on an LP.

By 1978 the group had definitely established itself as one of the most successful groups in the history of pop – and also as one of the wealthiest.

Thank you for the music

Words and music: Benny Andersson — Björn Ulvaeus

I'm nothing spe—cial, in fact I'm a bit— of a bore— If

I tell a joke— you've probab-ly heard— it be-fore— But

I have a ta——lent, a won-der-ful thing— 'cause eve-ry-one lis—tens when

I start to sing— I'm so grateful and proud all I want—

is to sing— it out loud— So I say thank you for the music, the

song I'm sing-ing. Thanks for all the joy they're bring-ing. Who can live without it? I

ask in all hones-ty— What would life be— without a song— or dance what are

we? So I say thank you for the music, for giv-ing it to me—

I've been so lucky I am the girl— with gol-den

hair. I wanna sing— it out— to eve-ry-bo-dy. What a joy, what a life, what a chance— CODA

So I say thank you for the music, for giv-ing it to me.

2 Mother says I was a
  dancer before I could walk.
  She says I began
  to sing long before I could talk
  And I've often wondered:
  How did it all start,
  who found out that nothing can
  capture a heart
  like a melody can?
  Well, who ever it was,
  I'm a fan.

  So I say
  Thank you for the music,
  the songs I'm singing.
  Thanks for all the
  joy they're bringing.
  Who can live without it?
  I ask in all honesty.
  What would life be
  without a song or dance,
  what are we?
  So I say
  thank you for the music,
  for giving it to me.

  I've been so lucky.
  I am the girl with golden hair.
  I wanna sing it out to everybody
  What a joy, what a life,
  what a chance.

  Thank you for the music . . .

  . . . for giving it to me.
  So I say
  thank you for the music,
  for giving it to me.

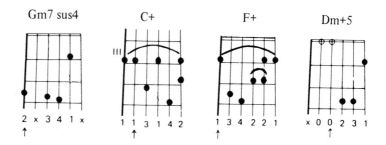

Gm7 sus4   C+   F+   Dm+5

2 x 3 4 1 x   1 1 3 1 4 2   1 3 4 2 2 1   x 0 0 2 3 1

Morning has broken

Words: Eleanor Farjeon
Music: Cat Stevens

Calmly

Mor - ning has bro - ken like the first mor————ning.

Black - bird has spo - ken like the first bird.

Praise for the sing - ing, praise for the mor - ning.

Praise for them spring - ing fresh from the word.

Note: Should be sung one octave lower than indicated by the music!

2 Sweet the rain's new fall,
sunlit from heaven.
Like the first dewfall
on the first grass.
Praise for the sweetness
of the wet garden.
Sprung in completeness
where his feet pass.

3 Mine is the sunlight,
mine is the morning.
Born of the one light
Eden saw play.
Praise with elation.
Praise ev'ry morning.
God's recreation
of the new day.

Prelude for piano

Interval and coda for piano

CAT STEVENS

Cat Stevens (whose real name is Steve Adams Georgiou) was born in London on
21 July 1948. His father is Greek-Cypriot and his mother Swedish. His first single 'I
love my dog', came out in 1966 and was a big hit in the charts, as were several subse-
quent songs such as 'Matthew and Son'. When he was 19 and fully embarked on his
career, he was struck down by tuberculosis and had to give up work for almost two
years. He made a come-back and did so with even better lyrics and music — and among
these are a large number which have come to be regarded as modern pop classics, for
example 'Morning has broken', 'Can't keep it in', 'Moonshadow' and 'Father and Son'.

Yes Sir, I can boogie

Words and music: Rolf Soja

Mis - ter / your eyes are full of hes - i - ta - tion
No sir, / I don't feel ve - ry much like talk - ing

Sure makes me won - der / if you know what you're look - ing for
No, nei - ther walk - ing / you— wan - na know if I can dance

Ba - by, / I wan - na keep my re - pu - ta - tion
Yes sir, / al - read - y told you in the first place

I'm a sen - sa - tion / You try me once, you'll beg for more.
and in the cho - rus / but I will give you one more chance.

Oh, Yes sir, I can boogie but I need a certain song—
Oh, Yes sir, I can boogie if you stay, you can't go wrong—

I can boogie boog - ie woogie, all night

long———

BACCARA

The story of Baccara began at a hotel on the Spanish island of Fuente Ventura in the Canary Islands, where Maria Mendiolo and Mayte Matheos, two Spanish girls from a Spanish television dance group, were performing. Three men from a German record company were staying at the hotel and when they heard the girls they at once decided to launch them.

A week later Maria and Mayte were in Hamburg, where a record producer, Rolf Soja, had specially written a song for them called 'Yes Sir, I can boogie'. The girls were launched under the name 'Baccara'. 'Yes Sir, I can boogie' was a success all over Europe and it was followed by new singles, including 'No Sir, I'm a lady' and also by LPs.

Moviestar

Words and music: Harpo

INSTR.

1. You feel like Steve — Mc - Queen when you're driv - ing in your car —

(3rd verse as far as ⊕)

And you think — you look — like James Bond when you're smoking your ci - gar, — it's so bi - zarre —

— You think you are — a new kind of — James Dean, but the on - ly thing I've

ev - er seen of you — was the commer — - cial spot — on the screen —

Mo - vie - star — oh mov — - vie - star — you think you are — a mov - - ie

Mo - vie - star — oh mov — - ie - star — you think you are — a mov — - ie -

star. Ah - a - a — INSTR.

2 You should belong to the jetset,
   fly your own private Lear-jet.
   But you worked in a grocery store every day
   until you could afford to get away.

   So you went to Sweden
   to meet Ingmar Bergman, he wasn't there,
   or he just didn't care.
   I think it's time for you, my friend
   to stop pretending that you are a
   moviestar, a moviestar.
   You think you are a movie,
   moviestar, a moviestar.
   You think you are a moviestar.
   Ah — a — a

3 Frozen hero
   your words are zero
   and your dreams
   have vanished into dark and long ago
   but you will want to know

   Oh, moviestar, oh moviestar
   you think you are a movie,
   moviestar, a moviestar.
   You think you are a moviestar.
   Ah — a — a

Note that the words of verses 2 and 3 differ
from the notes and that verse 3 is only half
the length of the rest.

HARPO

Harpo was born in 1950 and comes from
Stockholm. He began to write hits at an
early age and has composed over 200 songs
in all. He developed his stage technique
during his two years at drama school. He has
also worked as a producer, has written 18
plays for children (half of which have been
performed), is the author of two books and
has filled 'at least two wardrobes' with
poetry.

He had his big international break-
through with his hit 'Moviestar' in 1975. It
gave him the opportunity to make 18 television recordings in France, and even more
in Germany, Italy, Spain, Portugal, Holland,
Austria, Switzerland, East Germany and
England. He sold more than 2.5 million
records, among those 1.3 million in
Germany alone. That same year he and the
producer Bengt Palmers went to the USA,
where they together recorded the LP 'The
Hollywood Tapes'.

Harpo has also recorded 'Smile', which
was originally written by Charlie Chaplin for
the film 'Limelight'. You will find 'Smile'
on the next page.

Smile

Words and music: Chaplin — Turner — Parsons

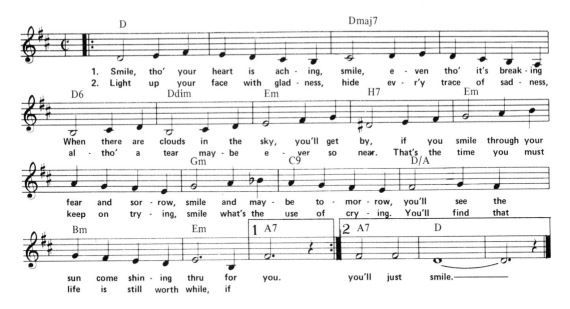

1. Smile, tho' your heart is ach - ing, smile, e - ven tho' it's break - ing
2. Light up your face with glad - ness, hide ev - r'y trace of sad - ness,

When there are clouds in the sky, you'll get by, if you smile through your
al - tho' a tear may - be e - ver so near. That's the time you must

fear and sor - row, smile and may - be to - mor - row, you'll see the
keep on try - ing, smile what's the use of cry - ing. You'll find that

sun come shin - ing thru for you. you'll just smile.
life is still worth while, if

Chorus backing

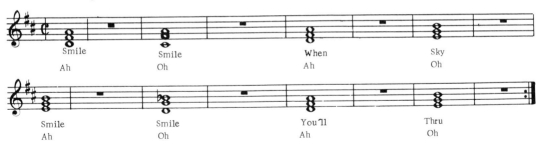

Smile   Smile   When   Sky
Ah   Oh   Ah   Oh

Smile   Smile   You'll   Thru
Ah   Oh   Ah   Oh

Charles Chaplin

L'été Indien

Words and music: Ward — Losito — Pallavicini — Cutugno — Delanoe — Lemesle

On i - ra——— ou tu voudras quand tu voudras———

Et l'on s'ai - me - ra en - core——— lorsque l'a - mour sera mort Tout' la vie——— se - ra pareille à

ce matin——— Aux couleurs——— de l'été In - dien.———

The words of this song say:
We will go where you want, when you want and we'll love each other again until love
dies. All life will be like that morning — in the colours of the Indian summer.

The melody can be performed like this:

1 One person recites the text, the rest hum the melody.
2 One person recites the text, some sing the unison part and one instrument plays
the melody.

Unison

Example of the piano accompaniment

I'm not in love

Words and music: Eric Stewart — Graham Gouldman

Note: should be sung one octave lower than indicated by the music!

2 I like to see you,
   but then again,
   that doesn't mean
   you mean that much to me.
   So if I call you,
   don't make a fuss.
   Don't tell your friends
   about the two of us.
   I'm not in love,
   no, no!
   It's because.

3 I keep your picture
   upon the wall.
   It hides a nasty stain
   that's lying there.
   So don't you ask me
   to give it back.
   I know you know
   it doesn't mean that much to me.
   I'm not in love,
   no, no!
   It's because.

   Ooh, you'll wait a long time
   for me.
   Ooh, you'll wait a long time.
   Ooh, you'll wait a long time
   for me.
   Ooh, you'll wait a long time.

4 I'm not in love,
   so don't forget it.
   It's just a silly phase
   I'm going through.
   And just because
   I call you up.
   Don't get me wrong,
   don't think you've got it made.
   I'm not in love,
   I'm not in love.

10 CC

10 CC's music has been described as intelligent, satirical, professional and completely crazy.

Their first single 'Donna' came out in 1972 but the members of the group at that time — Lol Creme, Kevin Godley, Graham Gouldman and Eric Stewart, had all individually had long experience of the pop world before that date. Together they became one of the greatest and most highly acclaimed pop-groups in the world with hits such as 'Donna', 'Wall Street Shuffle' and 'Rubber Bullets'.

In 1973 they were joined by a new member, Paul Burgess, who played the drums. In 1975 camp the LP 'The Original Soundtrack', which included the hit 'I'm not in love', which was chosen 'Best single of the year' and is still regarded as something of a masterpiece today.

The next LP 'How dare you' included many good hits including 'I'm Mandy fly me' and 'Art for art's sake'.

At the end of 1976, 10 CC was re-formed when Lol Creme and Kevin Godley left to devote themselves to the 'Gizmo', an instrument they had invented and which they later introduced in a four-LP album. Eric Stewart, Graham Gouldman and Paul Burgess continued together and produced the LP 'Deceptive bends', which included 'The things we do for love' and 'Good morning Judge'. Three new members joined: Rich Fenn, Stuart Tosh and Tony O'Malley, and so far they have made two LPs together: 'Live and let live' and 'Bloody tourists'.

Eric Stewart and Graham Gouldman

43

Common chords

In this table you'll find the commonest chords in six major scales and six minor scales.

↑ indicates fundamental note of the chord.

x indicates that the string must be muffled or not played.

Roman numerals indicate frets.

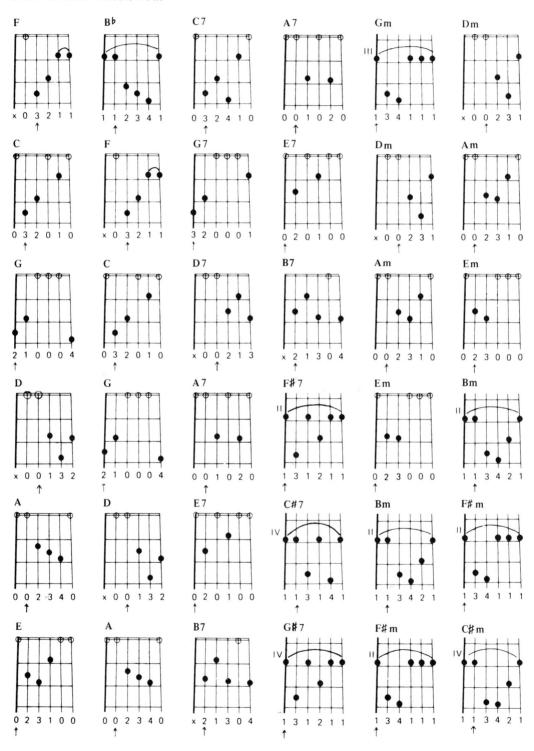

44

Barré chords

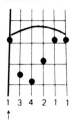

I	F
II	F#
III	G
IV	Ab
V	A
VI	Bb
VII	B
VIII	C
IX	C#
X	D

1 3 4 2 1 1

I	Fm
II	F#m
III	Gm
IV	G#m
V	Am
VI	Bbm
VII	Bm
VIII	Cm
IX	C#m
X	Dm

1 3 4 1 1 1

Sevenths
Lift your fourth finger and you get the corresponding major and minor 7th chord.

I, II etc: roman figures indicate the fret on the fingerboard of the guitar.

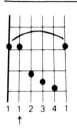

I	Bb
II	B
III	C
IV	C#
V	D
VI	D#
VII	E
VIII	F
IX	F#
X	G

1 1 2 3 4 1

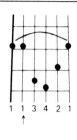

I	Bbm
II	Bm
III	Cm
IV	C#m
V	Dm
VI	D#m
VII	Em
VIII	Fm
IX	F#m
X	Gm

1 1 3 4 2 1

Lift your third finger for major 7th chord.
Lift your fourth finger for minor 7th chord.

Diminished chords

x x 1 3 2 4

Diminished chords without barré.

I	F#dim (A, C, Eb, D#)
II	G dim (Bb, C#, E)
III	F dim (Ab, G#, H, D)
IV	F#dim
	etc.

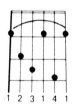

1 2 3 1 4 1

Diminished chords with barré.

I	F dim (Ab, G#, H, D)
II	F#dim (A, C, Eb, D#)
III	G dim (Bb, C#, E)
IV	F dim
	etc.

More unusual chords

These chords can be played up and down the fretboard (the keys changing by semitones accordingly).

(Eb)maj7

1 4 4 4

(Bb)maj7

1 1 3 2 4 1

(Bb)6
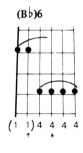

(1 1) 4 4 4 4

(F)6

1 3 x 2 4 1

(E)m7-5
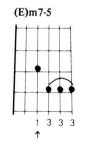

1 3 3 3

(Bb)M7-5
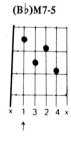

x 1 3 2 4 x

(F)7sus4
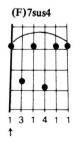

1 3 1 4 1 1

(Bb)7sus4

1 1 3 1 4 1

(B)9
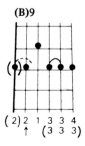

(2) 2 1 3 3 4
(3 3 3)

(F)9

1 3 1 2 1 4

(F♮)7-5
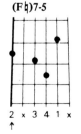

2 x 3 4 1 x

(F)13

1 x 1 2 4(1)

ACKNOWLEDGEMENTS

The publishers would like to thank the following for permission to reproduce music and lyrics in their copyright:

p. 6 *You are the sunshine of my life* Jobete Music Company Inc

p. 8 *Streets of London* Words and Music by Ralph McTell. Reproduced by permission of Essex Music International Ltd

p. 10 *How deep is your love* Words and Music by Barry, Robin and Maurice Gibb © 1977 Brothers BV British Publisher: RSO Publishing Lrd (Chappell Music Ltd)

p. 12 *Walk right in* by Gus Cannon and Hosea Woods, Southern Music Publishing Company Ltd

p. 14 *Sailing*, p. 26 *You can get it if you really want*, and p. 34 *Morning has broken*, Island Music

p. 16 *Border song* by Elton John and Bernie Taupin © 1969 World by Dick James Music Limited – London (All Rights Reserved)

p. 18 *Let it be* and p. 20 *When I'm sixty-four*, ATV Music

p. 23 *My sweet Lord* by George Harrison, Peter Maurice Music Co. Ltd/Harrisongs Ltd

p. 24 *Ain't that just the way*, MCA Music Ltd

p. 28 *By the rivers of Babylon*, ATV Music/Island Music

p. 30 *Money, money, money* and p. 32 *Thank you for the music* by Andersson and Ulvaeus, BOCU Music Ltd

p. 36 *Yes sir, I can boogie* by Rolf Soia and Frank Dostal, Louvigny Music Co Ltd

p. 40 *Smile* by Chaplin, Turner and Parsons, Bourne Music Ltd

p. 42 *I'm not in love* St Annes Music Ltd

Photographs supplied by the publishers as shown above except for p. 21 EMI Records.